"There are few poets writing in America today who share his lavish appetite for the bizarre, his inexhaustible repertoire of indelible characters and gestures... Simic is perhaps our most disquieting muse."   —*Harvard Review*

Praise for NIGHT PICNIC

"No other contemporary poet has such a brilliantly quirky sensibility. Only Simic could offer—in the same volume—themes of longing, heartache and intense soul-searching alongside dissections of life's absurdities and minutiae."
                                    —*The San Diego Union-Tribune*

"Simic has been working for more than four decades at his art, and he's brushed up against perfection more than a few times. Indeed, American poetry would be desperately poorer without at least a dozen of his poems."   —*The Nation*

"Simic creates a closely observed world bristling with emotion and significance."   —*Time Out New York*

Praise for JACKSTRAWS

"Simic is a master at interrogating ordinary occurrences with piercing yet slightly tongue-in-cheek observations."
                                    —*The New York Times Book Review*

"The poems are like self-developing Polaroids, in which a scene, gradually assembling itself out of unexplained images, suddenly clicks into a recognizable whole." —*The New York Review of Books*

The Voice at 3:00 A.M.

The Voice at 3:00 A.M.

Selected Late & New Poems

Charles Simic

A HARVEST BOOK
HARCOURT, INC.

Orlando ★ *Austin* ★ *New York* ★ *San Diego* ★ *Toronto* ★ *London*

Copyright © 2003 by Charles Simic

www.HarcourtBooks.com

The Library of Congress has cataloged the hardcover edition as follows:
Simic, Charles, 1938–
The voice at 3:00 A.M.: selected late and new poems / Charles Simic.
p. cm.
I. Title: Voice at 3:00 A.M. II. Title.
PS3569.I4725V6 2003
811'.54—dc21 2002038715
ISBN-13: 978-0-15-100842-1 ISBN-10: 0-15-100842-6
ISBN-13: 978-0-15-603073-1 (pbk.) ISBN-10: 0-15-603073-X (pbk.)

Text set in Dante
Designed by Scott Piehl

Printed in the United States of America

First Harvest edition 2006
A C E G I K J H F D B

To Helen

CONTENTS

From *Unending Blues*, 1986

DECEMBER

It snows
and still the derelicts
 go
carrying sandwich boards—

 one proclaiming
the end of the world
 the other
the rates of a local barbershop.

EARLY EVENING ALGEBRA

The madwoman went marking X's
With a piece of school chalk
On the backs of unsuspecting
Hand-holding, homebound couples.

It was winter. It was dark already.
One could not see her face
Bundled up as she was and furtive.
She went as if wind-swept, as if crow-winged.

The chalk must have been given to her by a child.
One kept looking for him in the crowd,
Expecting him to be very pale, very serious,
With a chip of black slate in his pocket.

TOWARD NIGHTFALL

for Don and Jane

The weight of tragic events
On everyone's back,
Just as tragedy
In the proper Greek sense
Was thought impossible
To compose in our day.

There were scaffolds,
Makeshift stages,
Puny figures on them,
Like small indistinct animals
Caught in the headlights
Crossing the road way ahead,

In the gray twilight
That went on hesitating
On the verge of a huge
Starless autumn night.
One could've been in
The back of an open truck
Hunkering because of
The speed and chill.

One could've been walking
With a sidelong glance
At the many troubling shapes
The bare trees made—
Like those about to shriek,

But finding themselves unable
To utter a word now.

One could've been in
One of these dying mill towns
Inside a small dim grocery
When the news broke.
One would've drawn near the radio
With the one many months pregnant
Who serves there at that hour.

Was there a smell of
Spilled blood in the air,
Or was it that other,
Much finer scent—of fear,
The fear of approaching death
One met on the empty street?

Monsters on movie posters, too,
Prominently displayed.
Then, six factory girls,
Arm in arm, laughing
As if they've been drinking.
At the very least, one
Could've been one of them.

The one with a mouth
Painted bright red,
Who feels out of sorts,
For no reason, very pale,
And so, excusing herself,
Vanishes where it says:
Rooms for Rent,
And immediately goes to bed,
Fully dressed, only

To lie with eyes open,
Trembling, despite the covers.
It's just a bad chill,
She keeps telling herself
Not having seen the papers
Which the landlord has the dog
Bring from the front porch.

The old man never learned
To read well, and so
Reads on in that half-whisper,
And in that half-light
Verging on the dark,
About that day's tragedies
Which supposedly are not
Tragedies in the absence of
Figures endowed with
Classic nobility of soul.

WILLIAM AND CYNTHIA

Says she'll take him to the Museum
Of Dead Ideas and Emotions.
Wonders that he hasn't been there yet.
Says it looks like a Federal courthouse
With its many steps and massive columns.

Apparently not many people go there
On such drizzly gray afternoons.
Says even she gets afraid
In the large empty exhibition halls
With monstrous ideas in glass cases,
Naked emotions on stone pedestals
In classically provocative poses.

Says she doesn't understand why he claims
All that reminds him of a country fair.
Admits there's a lot of old dust
And the daylight is the color of sepia,
Just like on this picture postcard
With its two lovers chastely embracing
Against a painted cardboard sunset.

AT THE NIGHT COURT

You've combed yourself carefully,
Your Honor, with a small fine-tooth comb
You then cleverly concealed
Before making your entrance
In the splendor of your black robes.

The comb tucked inside a handkerchief
Scented with the extract of dead roses—
While you took your high seat
Sternly eyeing each of the accused
In the hush of the empty courtroom.

The dark curly hairs in the comb
Did not come from your graying head.
One of the cleaning women used it on herself
While you dozed off in your chambers
Half undressed because of the heat.

The black comb in the pocket over the heart,
You feel it tremble just as ours do
When they ready themselves to make music
Lacking only the paper you're signing,
By the looks of it, with eyes closed.

FIRST FROST

The time of the year for the mystics.
October sky and the Cloud of Unknowing.
The routes of eternity beckoning.
Sign and enigma in the humblest of things.

Master cobbler Jakob Boehme
Sat in our kitchen all morning.
He sipped tea and warned of the quiet
To which the wise must school themselves.

The young woman paid no attention.
Hair fallen over her eyes,
Breasts loose and damp in her robe,
Stubbornly scrubbing a difficult stain.

Then the dog's bark brought us all outdoors,
And that wasn't just geese honking,
But Dame Julian of Norwich herself discoursing
On the marvelous courtesy and homeliness of the Maker.

FOR THE SAKE OF AMELIA

Tending a cliff-hanging Grand Hotel
In a country ravaged by civil war.
My heart as its only bellhop.
My brain as its Chinese cook.

It's a run-down seaside place
With a row of gutted limousines out front,
Monkeys and fighting cocks in the great ballroom,
Potted palm trees grown wild to the ceilings.

Amelia surrounded by her beaus and fortune-tellers,
Painting her eyelashes and lips blue
In the hour of dusk with the open sea beyond,
The long empty beaches, the tide's shimmer...

She pleading with me to check the ledgers,
Find out if Lenin stayed here once,
Buster Keaton, Nathaniel Hawthorne,
St. Bernard of Clairvaux, who wrote on love?

A hotel in which one tangos to a silence
Which has the look of cypresses in silent films...
In which children confide to imaginary friends...
In which pages of an important letter are flying...

But now a buzz from the suite with mirrors.
Amelia in the nude, black cotton over her eyes.
It seems there's a fly
On the tip of her lover's Roman nose.

Night of distant guns, distant and comfortable.
I am coming with a flyswatter on a silver tray.
Ah the Turkish delights!
And the Mask of Tragedy over her pubic hair.

OCTOBER ARRIVING

I only have a measly ant
To think with today.
Others have pictures of saints,
Others have clouds in the sky.

The winter might be at the door,
For he's all alone
And in a hurry to hide.
Nevertheless, unable to decide

He retraces his steps
Several times and finds himself
On a huge blank wall
That has no window.

Dark masses of trees
Cast their mazes before him,
Only to erase them next
With a sly, sea-surging sound.

AGAINST WHATEVER IT IS THAT'S ENCROACHING

Best of all is to be idle,
And especially on a Thursday,
And to sip wine while studying the light:
The way it ages, yellows, turns ashen
And then hesitates forever
On the threshold of the night
That could be bringing the first frost.

It's good to have a woman around just then,
And two is even better.
Let them whisper to each other
And eye you with a smirk.
Let them roll up their sleeves and unbutton their shirts a bit
As this fine old twilight deserves,

And the small schoolboy
Who has come home to a room almost dark
And now watches wide-eyed
The grown-ups raise their glasses to him,
The giddy-headed, red-haired woman
With eyes tightly shut,
As if she were about to cry or sing.

PROMISES OF LENIENCY AND FORGIVENESS

Orphanage in the rain,
Empty opera house with its light dimmed,
Thieves' market closed for the day,
O evening sky with your cloudy tableaus!

Incurable romantic marrying eternal grumblers.
Life haunted by its more beautiful sister life—
Always, always . . . We had nothing
But words. Someone rising to eloquence

After a funeral, or in the naked arms of a woman
Who has her head averted because she's crying,
And doesn't know why. A hairline fracture of the soul
Because of the way light falls on these bare trees and bushes.

Sea-blackened rocks inscrutable as chess players . . .
One spoke to them of words failing . . .
Of great works and little faith, of blues in each bite of bread.
Above the clouds the firm No went on pacing.

The woman had a tiny smile and an open umbrella,
Since now it had started to rain in a whisper,
The kind of rain that must've whispered in some other life
Of which we know nothing anymore except

That someone kept watching it come down softly,
Already soot-colored to make them think of
Serious children at play, and of balls of lint in a dark corner
Like wigs, fright wigs for the infinite.

From *The Book of Gods and Devils,* 1990

THE LITTLE PINS OF MEMORY

There was a child's Sunday suit
Pinned to a tailor's dummy
In a dusty store window.
The store looked closed for years.

I lost my way there once
In a Sunday kind of quiet,
Sunday kind of afternoon light
On a street of red-brick tenements.

How do you like that?
I said to no one.
How do you like that?
I said it again today upon waking.

That street went on forever
And all along I could feel the pins
In my back, prickling
The dark and heavy cloth.

ST. THOMAS AQUINAS

I left parts of myself everywhere
The way absent-minded people leave
Gloves and umbrellas
Whose colors are sad from dispensing so much bad luck.

I was on a park bench asleep.
It was like the Art of Ancient Egypt.
I didn't wish to bestir myself.
I made my long shadow take the evening train.

"We give death to a child when we give it a doll,"
Said the woman who had read Djuna Barnes.
We whispered all night. She had traveled to darkest Africa.
She had many stories to tell about the jungle.

I was already in New York looking for work.
It was raining as in the days of Noah.
I stood in many doorways of that great city.
Once I asked a man in a tuxedo for a cigarette.
He gave me a frightened look and stepped out into the rain.

Since "man naturally desires happiness,"
According to St. Thomas Aquinas,
Who gave irrefutable proof of God's existence and purpose,
I loaded trucks in the Garment Center.
A black man and I stole a woman's red dress.
It was of silk; it shimmered.

Upon a gloomy night with all our loving ardors on fire,
We carried it down the long empty avenue,
Each holding one sleeve.
The heat was intolerable causing many terrifying human faces
To come out of hiding.

In the Public Library Reading Room
There was a single ceiling fan barely turning.
I had the travels of Herman Melville to serve me as a pillow.
I was on a ghost ship with its sails fully raised.
I could see no land anywhere.
The sea and its monsters could not cool me.

I followed a saintly-looking nurse into a doctor's office.
We edged past people with eyes and ears bandaged.
"I am a medieval philosopher in exile,"
I explained to my landlady that night.
And, truly, I no longer looked like myself.
I wore glasses with a nasty spider crack over one eye.

I stayed in the movies all day long.
A woman on the screen walked through a bombed city
Again and again. She wore army boots.
Her legs were long and bare. It was cold wherever she was.
She had her back turned to me, but I was in love with her.
I expected to find wartime Europe at the exit.

It wasn't even snowing! Everyone I met
Wore a part of my destiny like a carnival mask.
"I'm Bartleby the Scrivener," I told the Italian waiter.
"Me, too," he replied.
And I could see nothing but overflowing ashtrays
The human-faced flies were busy examining.

A LETTER

Dear philosophers, I get sad when I think.
Is it the same with you?
Just as I'm about to sink my teeth into the noumenon,
Some old girlfriend comes to distract me.
"She's not even alive!" I yell to the skies.

The wintry light made me go that way.
I saw beds covered with identical gray blankets.
I saw grim-looking men holding a naked woman
While they hosed her with cold water.
Was that to calm her nerves, or was it punishment?

I went to visit my friend Bob, who said to me:
"We reach the real by overcoming the seduction of images."
I was overjoyed, until I realized
Such abstinence will never be possible for me.
I caught myself looking out the window.

Bob's father was taking their dog for a walk.
He moved with pain; the dog waited for him.
There was no one else in the park,
Only bare trees with an infinity of tragic shapes
To make thinking difficult.

FACTORY

The machines were gone, and so were those who worked them.
A single high-backed chair stood like a throne
In all that empty space.
I was on the floor making myself comfortable
For a long night of little sleep and much thinking.

An empty birdcage hung from a steam pipe.
In it I kept an apple and a small paring knife.
I placed newspapers all around me on the floor
So I could jump at the slightest rustle.
It was like the scratching of a pen,
The silence of the night writing in its diary.

Of rats who came to pay me a visit
I had the highest opinion.
They'd stand on two feet
As if about to make a polite request
On a matter of great importance.

Many other strange things came to pass.
Once a naked woman climbed on the chair
To reach the apple in the cage.
I was on the floor watching her go on tiptoe,
Her hand fluttering in the cage like a bird.

On other days, the sun peeked through dusty windowpanes
To see what time it was. But there was no clock,
Only the knife in the cage, glinting like a mirror,
And the chair in the far corner
Where someone once sat facing the brick wall.

SHELLEY

for M. Follain

Poet of the dead leaves driven like ghosts,
Driven like pestilence-stricken multitudes,
I read you first
One rainy evening in New York City,

In my atrocious Slavic accent,
Saying the mellifluous verses
From a battered, much-stained volume
I had bought earlier that day
In a secondhand bookstore on Fourth Avenue
Run by an initiate of the occult masters.

The little money I had being almost spent,
I walked the streets, my nose in the book.
I sat in a dingy coffee shop
With last summer's dead flies on the table.
The owner was an ex-sailor
Who had grown a huge hump on his back
While watching the rain, the empty street.
He was glad to have me sit and read,
He'd refill my cup with a liquid dark as river Styx.

Shelley spoke of a mad, blind, dying king;
Of rulers who neither see, nor feel, nor know;
Of graves from which a glorious Phantom may
Burst to illumine our tempestuous day.

I too felt like a glorious phantom
Going to have my dinner
In a Chinese restaurant I knew so well.
It had a three-fingered waiter
Who'd bring my soup and rice each night
Without ever saying a word.

I never saw anyone else there.
The kitchen was separated by a curtain
Of glass beads which clicked faintly
Whenever the front door opened.
The front door opened that evening
To admit a pale little girl with glasses.

The poet spoke of the everlasting universe
Of things . . . of gleams of a remoter world
Which visit the soul in sleep . . .
Of a desert peopled by storms alone . . .

The streets were strewn with broken umbrellas
Which looked like funereal kites
This little Chinese girl might have made.
The bars on MacDougal Street were emptying.
There had been a fistfight.
A man leaned against a lamppost arms extended as if crucified,
The rain washing the blood off his face.

In a dimly lit side street,
Where the sidewalk shone like a ballroom mirror
At closing time—

A well-dressed man without any shoes
Asked me for money.
His eyes shone, he looked triumphant
Like a fencing master
Who had just struck a mortal blow.

How strange it all was ... The world's raffle
That dark October night ...
The yellowed volume of poetry
With its Splendors and Glooms
Which I studied by the light of storefronts:
Drugstores and barbershops,
Afraid of my small windowless room
Cold as a tomb of an infant emperor.

THE BETROTHAL

I found a key
In the street, someone's
House key
Lying there, glinting,

Long ago. The one
Who lost it
Is not going to remember it
Tonight, as I do.

It was a huge city
Of many dark windows,
Many dark doorways.
I stood there thinking.

The street ahead of me
Shadowy, full of peril
Now that I held
The key. One or two

Late strollers in view,
Unhurried and grave.
The sky above them
Of an unearthly clarity.

Eternity jealous
Of the present moment,
It occurred to me!
And then the moment was over.

THE DEVILS

You were a "victim of semiromantic anarchism
In its most irrational form."
I was "ill at ease in an ambiguous world

Deserted by Providence." We drank wine
And made love in the afternoon. The neighbors'
TVs were tuned to soap operas.

The unhappy couples spoke little.
There were interminable pauses.
Soft organ music. Someone coughing.

"It's like Strindberg's *Dream Play*," you said.
"What is?" I asked and got no reply.
I was watching a spider on the ceiling.

It was the kind St. Veronica ate in her martyrdom.
"That woman subsisted on spiders only,"
I told the janitor when he came to fix the faucet.

He wore dirty overalls and a derby hat.
Once he had been an inmate of a notorious state institution.
"I'm no longer Jesus," he informed us happily.

He believed only in devils now.
"This building is full of them," he confided.
One could see their horns and tails

If one caught them in their baths.
"He's got Dark Ages on his brain," you said.
"Who does?" I asked and got no reply.

The spider had the beginnings of a web
Over our heads. The world was quiet
Except when one of us took a sip of wine.

EVENING TALK

Everything you didn't understand
Made you what you are. Strangers
Whose eye you caught on the street
Studying you. Perhaps they were the all-seeing
Illuminati? They knew what you didn't,
And left you troubled like a strange dream.

Not even the light stayed the same.
Where did all that hard glare come from?
And the scent, as if mythical beings
Were being groomed and fed stalks of hay
On these roofs drifting among the evening clouds.

You didn't understand a thing!
You loved the crowds at the end of the day
That brought you so many mysteries.
There was always someone you were meant to meet
Who for some reason wasn't waiting.
Or perhaps they were? But not here, friend.

You should have crossed the street
And followed that obviously demented woman
With the long streak of blood-red hair
Which the sky took up like a distant cry.

THE WHITE ROOM

The obvious is difficult
To prove. Many prefer
The hidden. I did, too.
I listened to the trees.

They had a secret
Which they were about to
Make known to me,
And then didn't.

Summer came. Each tree
On my street had its own
Scheherazade. My nights
Were a part of their wild

Storytelling. We were
Entering dark houses,
More and more dark houses
Hushed and abandoned.

There was someone with eyes closed
On the upper floors.
The thought of it, and the wonder,
Kept me sleepless.

The truth is bald and cold,
Said the woman
Who always wore white.
She didn't leave her room much.

The sun pointed to one or two
Things that had survived
The long night intact,
The simplest things,

Difficult in their obviousness.
They made no noise.
It was the kind of day
People describe as "perfect."

Gods disguising themselves
As black hairpins? A hand-mirror?
A comb with a tooth missing?
No! That wasn't it.

Just things as they are,
Unblinking, lying mute
In that bright light,
And the trees waiting for the night.

FRIGHTENING TOYS

History practicing its scissor-clips
In the dark,
So everything comes out in the end
Missing an arm or a leg.

Still, if that's all you've got
To play with today . . .
This doll at least had a head,
And its lips were red!

Frame houses like grim exhibits
Lining the empty street
Where a little girl sat on the steps
In a flowered nightgown, talking to it.

It looked like a serious matter,
Even the rain wanted to hear about it,
So it fell on her eyelashes,
And made them glisten.

THE BIG WAR

We played war during the war,
Margaret. Toy soldiers were in big demand,
The kind made from clay.
The lead ones they melted into bullets, I suppose.

You never saw anything as beautiful
As those clay regiments! I used to lie on the floor
For hours staring them in the eye.
I remember them staring back at me in wonder.

How strange they must have felt
Standing stiffly at attention
Before a large, incomprehending creature
With a moustache made of milk.

In time they broke, or I broke them on purpose.
There was wire inside their limbs,
Inside their chests, but nothing in the heads!
Margaret, I made sure.

Nothing at all in the heads ...
Just an arm, now and then, an officer's arm,
Wielding a saber from a crack
In my deaf grandmother's kitchen floor.

DEATH, THE PHILOSOPHER

He gives excellent advice by example.
"See!" he says. "See that?"
And he doesn't have to open his mouth
To tell you what.
You can trust his vast experience.
Still, there's no huff in him.
Once he had a most unfortunate passion.
It came to an end.
He loved the way the summer dusk fell.
He wanted to have it falling forever.
It was not possible.
That was the big secret.
It's dreadful when things get as bad as that—
But then they don't!
He got the point, and so, one day,
Miraculously lucid, you, too, came to ask
About the strangeness of it all.
Charles, you said,
How strange you should be here at all!

AT THE CORNER

The two fat sisters
Kept a candy store
Dim and narrow
With dusty jars
Of jaw-breaking candy.

We stayed thin, stayed
Glum, chewing gum
While staring at the shoes
Of men and women
Rushing in and out,

Making the newspapers
Outside flutter audibly
Under the lead weights,
Their headlines screaming
In and out of our view.

A WORD

Said by a child who doesn't know
The meaning of it. The neighbors
Coming to hear all about it,
But the door's locked. No one at home.

It's such a nice warm day
To be lost in a strange city.
The map of ancient Rome in your pocket,
Or is it Jerusalem?

"Please make him stop," she says.
We can only see her blood-red fingernails
Drying on the windowsill.
The one she's speaking to remains silent.

He's just an idea, anyway,
Sulking in some back room
With a somber view of its own. The child
Who cannot be put into words.

THE PIECES OF THE CLOCK LIE SCATTERED

So, hurry up!
The evening's coming.
The grown-ups are on the way.
There'll be hell to pay.

You forgot about time
While you sought its secret
In the slippery wheels,
Some of which had teeth.

You meant to enthrall
The girl across the hall.
She drew so near,
Her breast brushed your ear.

She ought to have gone home,
But you kept telling her
You'll have it together again
And ticking in no time.

Instead, you're under the table
Together, searching the floor.
Your hands are trembling,
And there's a key in the door.

THE IMMORTAL

You're shivering, O my memory.
You went out early and without a coat
To visit your old schoolmasters,
The cruel schoolmasters and their pet monkeys.
You took a wrong turn somewhere.
You met an army of gray days,
A ghost army of years on the march.
It was the bread they fed you,
The kind it takes a lifetime to chew.

You found yourself again on that street
Inside that small, rented room
With its single dusty window.
Outside it was snowing quietly,
Snowing and snowing for days on end.
You were ill and in bed.
Everyone else had gone to work.
The blind old woman next door,
Whose sighs and heavy steps you'd welcome now,
Had died mysteriously in the summer.

You had your own heartbeat to attend to.
You were perfectly alone and anonymous.
It would have taken months for anyone
To begin to miss you. The chill
Made you pull the covers up to your chin.

You remembered the lost arctic voyagers,
The evening snow erasing their footprints.

You had no money and no job.
Both of your lungs were hurting; still,
You had no intention of lifting a finger
To help yourself. You were immortal!

Outside, the same dark snowflake
Seemed to be falling over and over again.
You studied the cracked walls,
The maplike water stain on the ceiling,
Trying to fix in your mind its cities and rivers.

Time had stopped at dusk.
You were shivering at the thought
Of such great happiness.

THE GODS

The statues of Greek gods
In the storage room of the art school
Where I led Pamela by the hand,
Or was it she who led me?
Nibbled my ear, while I raised her skirt.

Identical Apollos held identical
Empty hands. Poor imitations,
I thought. They belong in a window
Of a store going out of business
On a street dark and desolate.

That's because my eyes were closed
Long before they were open again.
It was night. There was still light,
Enough to tell their nakedness from ours,
But I couldn't figure where it came from,
And how long it meant to stay.

TWO DOGS

for Charles and Holly

An old dog afraid of his own shadow
In some Southern town.
The story told me by a woman going blind,
One fine summer evening
As shadows were creeping
Out of the New Hampshire woods,
A long street with just a worried dog
And a couple of dusty chickens,
And all the sun beating down
In that nameless Southern town.

It made me remember the Germans marching
Past our house in 1944.
The way everybody stood on the sidewalk
Watching them out of the corner of the eye,
The earth trembling, death going by . . .
A little white dog ran into the street
And got entangled with the soldiers' feet.
A kick made him fly as if he had wings.
That's what I keep seeing!
Night coming down. A dog with wings.

CABBAGE

She was about to chop the head
In half,
But I made her reconsider
By telling her:
"Cabbage symbolizes mysterious love."

Or so said one Charles Fourier,
Who said many other strange and wonderful things,
So that people called him mad behind his back,

Whereupon I kissed the back of her neck
Ever so gently,

Whereupon she cut the cabbage in two
With a single stroke of her knife.

PARADISE

In a neighborhood once called "Hell's Kitchen"
Where a beggar claimed to be playing Nero's fiddle
While the city burned in midsummer heat;
Where a lady barber who called herself Cleopatra
Wielded the scissors of fate over my head
Threatening to cut off my ears and nose;
Where a man and a woman went walking naked
In one of the dark side streets at dawn.

I must be dreaming, I told myself.
It was like meeting a couple of sphinxes.
I expected them to have wings, bodies of lions:
Him with his wildly tattooed chest;
Her with her huge, dangling breasts.

It happened so quickly, and so long ago!

You know that time just before the day breaks
When one yearns to lie down on cool sheets
In a room with shades drawn?
The hour when the beautiful suicides
Lying side by side in the morgue
Get up and walk out into the first light.

The curtains of cheap hotels flying out of windows
Like seagulls, but everything else quiet . . .
Steam rising out of the subway gratings . . .
Bodies glistening with sweat . . .
Madness, and you might even say, paradise!

IN THE LIBRARY

for Octavio

There's a book called
A Dictionary of Angels.
No one had opened it in fifty years,
I know, because when I did,
The covers creaked, the pages
Crumbled. There I discovered

The angels were once as plentiful
As species of flies.
The sky at dusk
Used to be thick with them.
You had to wave both arms
Just to keep them away.

Now the sun is shining
Through the tall windows.
The library is a quiet place.
Angels and gods huddled
In dark unopened books.
The great secret lies
On some shelf Miss Jones
Passes every day on her rounds.

She's very tall, so she keeps
Her head tipped as if listening.
The books are whispering.
I hear nothing, but she does.

THE SCARECROW

God's refuted but the devil's not.

This year's tomatoes are something to see.
Bite into them, Martha,
As you would into a ripe apple.
After each bite add a little salt.

If the juices run down your chin
Onto your bare breasts,
Bend over the kitchen sink.

From there you can see your husband
Come to a dead stop in the empty field
Before one of his bleakest thoughts,
Spreading his arms like a scarecrow.

WINDY EVENING

This old world needs propping up
When it gets this cold and windy.
The cleverly painted sets,
Oh, they're shaking badly!
They're about to come down.

There'll be nothing but infinite space.
The silence supreme. Almighty silence.
Egyptian sky. Stars like torches
Of grave robbers entering the crypts of kings.
Even the wind pausing, waiting to see.

Better grab hold of that tree, Lucille.
Its shape crazed, terror-stricken.
I'll hold on to the barn.
The chickens in it are restless.
Smart chickens, rickety world.

From *Hotel Insomnia*, 1992

EVENING CHESS

The Black Queen raised high
In my father's angry hand.

THE CITY

At least one crucified at every corner.
The eyes of a mystic, madman, murderer.
They know it's truly for nothing.
The eyes do. All the martyr's sufferings
On parade. Exalted mother of us all
Tending her bundles on the sidewalk,
Speaking to each as if it were a holy child.

There were many who saw none of this.
A couple lingered on kissing lustily
Right where someone lay under a newspaper.
His bloody feet, swollen twice their size,
Jutted out into the cold of the day,
Grim proofs of a new doctrine.

I tell you, I was afraid. A man screamed
And continued walking as if nothing had happened.
Everyone whose eyes I sought avoided mine.
Was I beginning to resemble him a little?
I had no answer to any of these questions.
Neither did the crucified on the next corner.

PENAL ARCHITECTURE

School, prison, state orphanage,
I walked your gray hallways,
Stood in your darkest corners
With my face to the wall.

The murderer sat in the front row.
A mad little Ophelia
Wrote the date on the blackboard.
The executioner was my best friend.
He already wore black.

Cracked, peeling walls
With every window barred,
Not even a naked lightbulb
For the boy left in the solitary
And the old master
Putting on his eyeglasses.

In that room with its red sunsets,
It was eternity's turn to speak,
So we listened breathlessly
Even though our hearts
Were made of stone.

THE PRODIGAL

Dark morning rain
Meant to fall
On a prison and a school yard,
Falling meanwhile
On my mother and her old dog.

How slow she shuffles now
In my father's Sunday shoes.
The dog by her side
Trembling with each step
As he tries to keep up.

I am on another corner waiting
With my head shaved.
My mind hops like a sparrow
In the rain.
I'm always watching and worrying about her.

Everything is a magic ritual,
A secret cinema,
The way she appears in a window hours later
To set the empty bowl
And spoon on the table,
And then exits
So that the day may pass,
And the night may fall

Into the empty bowl,
Empty room, empty house,
While the rain keeps
Knocking at the front door.

HOTEL INSOMNIA

I liked my little hole,
Its window facing a brick wall.
Next door there was a piano.
A few evenings a month
A crippled old man came to play
"My Blue Heaven."

Mostly, though, it was quiet.
Each room with its spider in heavy overcoat
Catching his fly with a web
Of cigarette smoke and revery.
So dark,
I could not see my face in the shaving mirror.

At 5 A.M. the sound of bare feet upstairs.
The "Gypsy" fortuneteller,
Whose storefront is on the corner,
Going to pee after a night of love.
Once, too, the sound of a child sobbing.
So near it was, I thought
For a moment, I was sobbing myself.

THE TIGER

in memory of George Oppen

In San Francisco, that winter,
There was a dark little store
Full of sleepy Buddhas.
The afternoon I walked in,
No one came out to greet me.
I stood among the sages
As if trying to read their thoughts.

One was huge and made of stone.
A few were the size of a child's head
And had stains the color of dried blood.
There were some no bigger than mice,
And they appeared to be listening.

"The winds of March, black winds,
The gritty winds," the dead poet wrote.

At sundown his street was empty
Except for my long shadow
Open before me like scissors.
There was his house where I told the story
Of the Russian soldier,
The one who looked Chinese.

He lay wounded in my father's bed,
And I brought him water and matches.
For that he gave me a little tiger
Made of ivory. Its mouth was open in anger,
But it had no stripes left.

There was the night when I colored
Its eyes black, its tongue red.
My mother held the lamp for me,
While worrying about the kind of luck
This beast might bring us.

The tiger in my hand growled faintly
When we were alone in the dark,
But when I put my ear to the poet's door
That afternoon, I heard nothing.

"The winds of march, black winds,
The gritty winds," he once wrote.

CLOUDS GATHERING

It seemed the kind of life we wanted.
Wild strawberries and cream in the morning.
Sunlight in every room.
The two of us walking by the sea naked.

Some evenings, however, we found ourselves
Unsure of what comes next.
Like tragic actors in a theater on fire,
With birds circling over our heads,
The dark pines strangely still,
Each rock we stepped on bloodied by the sunset.

We were back on our terrace sipping wine.
Why always this hint of an unhappy ending?
Clouds of almost human appearance
Gathering on the horizon, but the rest lovely
With the air so mild and the sea untroubled.

The night suddenly upon us, a starless night.
You lighting a candle, carrying it naked
Into our bedroom and blowing it out quickly.
The dark pines and grasses strangely still.

FOLK SONGS

Sausage-makers of History,
The bloody kind,
You all hail from a village
Where the dog barking at the moon
Is the only poet.

*

O King Oedipus, O Hamlet,
Fallen like flies
In the pot of cabbage soup,
No use beating with your fists,
Or sticking your tongues out.

*

Christ-faced spider on the wall
Darkened by evening shadows,
I spent my childhood on a cross
In a yard full of weeds,
White butterflies, and white chickens.

A BOOK FULL OF PICTURES

Father studied theology through the mail
And this was exam time.
Mother knitted. I sat quietly with a book
Full of pictures. Night fell.
My hands grew cold touching the faces
Of dead kings and queens.

There was a black raincoat
      in the upstairs bedroom
Swaying from the ceiling,
But what was it doing there?
Mother's long needles made quick crosses.
They were black
Like the inside of my head just then.

The pages I turned sounded like wings.
"The soul is a bird," he once said.
In my book full of pictures
A battle raged: lances and swords
Made a kind of wintry forest
With my heart spiked and bleeding in its branches.

EVENING WALK

You give the appearance of listening
To my thoughts, O trees,
Bent over the road I am walking
On a late summer evening
When every one of you is a steep staircase
The night is slowly descending.

The high leaves like my mother's lips
Forever trembling, unable to decide,
For there's a bit of wind,
And it's like hearing voices,
Or a mouth full of muffled laughter,
A huge dark mouth we can all fit in
Suddenly covered by a hand.

Everything quiet. Light
Of some other evening strolling ahead,
Long-ago evening of silk dresses,
Bare feet, hair unpinned and falling.
Happy heart, what heavy steps you take
As you follow after them in the shadows.

The sky at the road's end cloudless and blue.
The night birds like children
Who won't come to dinner.
Lost children in the darkening woods.

HOTEL STARRY SKY

Millions of empty rooms with TV sets turned on.
I wasn't there yet I saw everything.
Titanic on the screen like a
    birthday cake sinking.
Poseidon, the night clerk, blew out the candles.

How much should we tip the blind bellhop?
At three in the morning the gum machine
    in the empty lobby
With its freshly cracked mirror
Is the new Madonna with her infant child.

TO THINK CLEARLY

What I need is a pig and an angel.
The pig to stick his nose in a slop bucket,
The angel to scratch his back
And say sweet things in his ear.

The pig knows what's in store for him.
Give him hope, angel child,
With that foreverness stuff.
Don't go admiring yourself
In the butcher's knife
As if it were a whore's mirror,
Or tease him with a bloodstained apron
By raising it above your knees.

The pig has stopped eating
And stands among us thinking.
Already the crest of the rooster blazes
In the morning darkness.
He's not crowing but his eyes are fierce
As he struts across the yard.

THE CHAIR

This chair was once a student of Euclid.

The book of his laws lay on its seat.
The schoolhouse windows were open,
So the wind turned the pages
Whispering the glorious proofs.

The sun set over the golden roofs.
Everywhere the shadows lengthened,
But Euclid kept quiet about that.

LOST GLOVE

Here's a woman's black glove.
It ought to mean something.
A thoughtful stranger left it
On the red mailbox at the corner.

Three days the sky was troubled,
Then today a few snowflakes fell
On the glove, which someone,
In the meantime, had turned over,
So that its fingers could close

A little . . . Not yet a fist.
So I waited, with the night coming.
Something told me not to move.
Here where flames rise from trash barrels,
And the homeless sleep standing up.

ROMANTIC SONNET

Evenings of sovereign clarity—
Wine and bread on the table,
Mother praying,
Father naked in bed.

Was I that skinny boy stretched out
In the field behind the house,
His heart cut out with a toy knife?
Was I the crow hovering over him?

Happiness, you are the bright red lining
Of the dark winter coat
Grief wears inside out.

This is about myself when I'm remembering,
And your long insomniac's nails,
O Time, I keep chewing and chewing.

BEAUTY

I'm telling you, this was the real thing, the same one they kicked out of Aesthetics, told her she didn't exist!

O you simple, indefinable, ineffable, and so forth. I like your black apron, and your new Chinese girl's hairdo. I also like naps in the afternoon, well-chilled white wine, and the squabbling of philosophers.

What joy and happiness you give us each time you reach over the counter to take our money, so we catch a whiff of your breath. You've been chewing on sesame crackers and garlic salami, divine creature!

When I heard the old man, Plotinus, say something about "every soul wanting to possess you," I gave him a dirty look, and rushed home to unwrap and kiss the pink ham you sliced for me with your own hand.

MY QUARREL WITH THE INFINITE

I preferred the fleeting,
Like a memory of a sip of wine
Of noble vintage
On the tongue with eyes closed . . .

When you tapped me on the shoulder,
O light, unsayable in your splendor.
A lot of good you did me.
You just made my insomnia last longer.

I sat rapt at the spectacle,
Secretly ruing the fugitive:
All its provisory, short-lived
Kisses and enchantments.

Here with the new day breaking,
And a single scarecrow on the horizon
Directing the traffic
Of crows and their shadows.

THE OLD WORLD

for Dan and Jeanne

I believe in the soul; so far
It hasn't made much difference.
I remember an afternoon in Sicily.
The ruins of some temple.
Columns fallen in the grass like naked lovers.

The olives and goat cheese tasted delicious
And so did the wine
With which I toasted the coming night,
The darting swallows,
The Saracen wind and moon.

It got darker. There was something
Long before there were words:
The evening meal of shepherds ...
A fleeting whiteness among the trees ...
Eternity eavesdropping on time.

The goddess going to bathe in the sea.
She must not be followed.
These rocks, these cypress trees,
May be her old lovers.
Oh to be one of them, the wine whispered to me.

COUNTRY FAIR

for Hayden Carruth

If you didn't see the six-legged dog,
It doesn't matter.
We did and he mostly lay in the corner.
As for the extra legs,

One got used to them quickly
And thought of other things.
Like, what a cold, dark night
To be out at the fair.

Then the keeper threw a stick
And the dog went after it
On four legs, the other two flapping behind,
Which made one girl shriek with laughter.

She was drunk and so was the man
Who kept kissing her neck.
The dog got the stick and looked back at us.
And that was the whole show.

From *A Wedding in Hell*, 1994

SINISTER COMPANY

Just the other day
On the busy street
You stopped to search your pockets
For some change
When you noticed them following you:

Blind, deaf, mad and homeless,
Out of respect keeping their distance.
You are our Emperor! they shouted.
Chief executioner!
The world's greatest tamer of wild beasts!

As for your pockets,
There was a hole in each one
At which they drew close
Touching you everywhere,
Raising a paper crown to your head.

DREAM AVENUE

Monumental, millennial decrepitude,
As tragedy requires. A broad
Avenue with trash unswept,
A few solitary speck-sized figures
Going about their business
In a world already smudged by a schoolboy's eraser.

You've no idea what city this is,
What country? It could be a dream,
But is it yours? You're nothing
But a vague sense of loss,
A piercing, heart-wrenching dread
On an avenue with no name

With a few figures conveniently small
And blurred who in any case
Have their backs to you
As they look elsewhere, beyond
The long row of gray buildings and their many windows,
Some of which appear to be broken.

PARADISE MOTEL

Millions were dead; everybody was innocent.
I stayed in my room. The President
Spoke of war as of a magic love potion.
My eyes were opened in astonishment.
In a mirror my face appeared to me
Like a twice-canceled postage stamp.

I lived well, but life was awful.
There were so many soldiers that day,
So many refugees crowding the roads.
Naturally, they all vanished
With a touch of the hand.
History licked the corners of its bloody mouth.

On the pay channel, a man and a woman
Were trading hungry kisses and tearing off
Each other's clothes while I looked on
With the sound off and the room dark
Except for the screen where the color
Had too much red in it, too much pink.

THE CLOCKS OF THE DEAD

One night I went to keep the clock company.
It had a loud tick after midnight
As if it were uncommonly afraid.
It's like whistling past a graveyard,
I explained.
In any case, I told him I understood.

Once there were clocks like that
In every kitchen in America.
Now the factory's windows are all broken.
The old men on night shift are in Charon's boat.
The day you stop, I said to the clock,
The little wheels they keep in reserve
Will have rolled away
Into many hard-to-find places.

Just thinking about it, I forgot to wind the clock.
We woke up in the dark.
How quiet the city is, I said.
Like the clocks of the dead, my wife replied.
Grandmother on the wall,
I heard the snows of your childhood
Begin to fall.

EXPLAINING A FEW THINGS

Every worm is a martyr,
Every sparrow subject to injustice,
I said to my cat,
Since there was no one else around.

It's raining. In spite of their huge armies
What can the ants do?
And the roach on the wall
Like a waiter in an empty restaurant?

I'm going down to the cellar
To stroke the rat caught in a trap.
You watch the sky.
If it clears, scratch on the door.

ROMANTIC LANDSCAPE

To grieve, always to suffer
At the thought of time passing.
The outside world shadowy
As your deepest self.
Melancholy meadows, trees so still,
They seem afraid of themselves.

The sunset sky for one brief moment
Radiant with some supreme insight,
And then it's over. Tragic theater:
Blood and mourning at which
Even the birds fall silent.

Spirit, you who are everywhere and nowhere,
Watch over the lost lamb
Now that the mouth of the Infinite
Opens over us
And its dumb tongue begins to move darkly.

LEAVES

Lovers who take pleasure
In the company of trees,
Who seek diversion after many kisses
In each other's arms,
Watching the leaves,

The way they quiver
At the slightest breath of wind,
The way they thrill,
And shudder almost individually,
One of them beginning to shake
While the others are still quiet,
Unaccountably, unreasonably—

What am I saying?
One leaf in a million more fearful,
More happy,
Than all the others?

On this oak tree casting
Such deep shade,
And my lids closing sleepily
With that one leaf twittering
Now darkly, now luminously.

TRANSPORT

In the frying pan
On the stove
I found my love
And me naked.

Chopped onions
Fell on our heads
And made us cry.
It's like a parade,
I told her, confetti
When some guy
Reaches the moon.

"Means of transport,"
She replied obscurely
While we fried.
"Means of transport!"

CRAZY ABOUT HER SHRIMP

We don't even take time
To come up for air.
We keep our mouths full and busy
Eating bread and cheese
And smooching in between.

No sooner have we made love
Than we are back in the kitchen.
While I chop the hot peppers,
She wiggles her ass
And stirs the shrimp on the stove.

How good the wine tastes
That has run red
Out of a laughing mouth!
Down her chin
And onto her naked tits.

"I'm getting fat," she says,
Turning this way and that way
Before the mirror.
"I'm crazy about her shrimp!"
I shout to the gods above.

READING HISTORY

for Hans Magnus

At times, reading here
In the library,
I'm given a glimpse
Of those condemned to death
Centuries ago,
And of their executioners.
I see each pale face before me
The way a judge
Pronouncing a sentence would,
Marveling at the thought
That I do not exist yet.

With eyes closed I can hear
The evening birds.
Soon they will be quiet
And the final night on earth
Will commence
In the fullness of its sorrow.

How vast, dark, and impenetrable
Are the early-morning skies
Of those led to their death
In a world from which I'm entirely absent,
Where I can still watch
Someone's slumped back,

Someone who is walking away from me
With his hands tied,
His graying head still on his shoulders,

Someone who
In what little remains of his life
Knows in some vague way about me,
And thinks of me as God,
As Devil.

EMPIRES

My grandmother prophesied the end
Of your empires, O fools!
She was ironing. The radio was on.
The earth trembled beneath our feet.

One of your heroes was giving a speech.
"Monster," she called him.
There were cheers and gun salutes for the monster.
"I could kill him with my bare hands,"
She announced to me.

There was no need to. They were all
Going to the devil any day now.
"Don't go blabbering about this to anyone,"
She warned me.
And pulled my ear to make sure I understood.

THE TOWER

Five, six chairs piled up in the yard
And you on top of them
Sitting like a hanging judge,
Wearing only pajama bottoms.

The sparrows, what must they think?
If people are watching,
They are as quiet as goldfish,
Or expensive cuts of meat.

Hour after hour alone with the sky
And its mad serenity
On the rickety, already teetering,
Already leaning tower.

How frightened the neighbors must be.
Not even a child walks the streets
In this heat,
Not even a car passes and slows down.

What do you see in the distance, O father?
A windowpane struck by the setting sun?
A game called on account of darkness?
The players like fleas in a convent.

Hell's bells about to toll?

SHAVING

Child of sorrow.
Old snotnose.
Stray scrap from the table of the gods.
Toothless monkey.
Workhorse,
Wheezing there,
Coughing too.

The trouble with you is,
Your body and soul
Don't get along well together.
Pigsty for a brain,
Stop them from making faces at each other
In the mirror!
Then, remove the silly angel wings
From your gorilla suit.

MYSTICS

Help me to find what I've lost,
If it was ever, however briefly, mine,
You who may have found it.
Old man praying in the privy,
Lonely child drawing a secret room
And in it a stopped clock.

Seek to convey its truth to me
By hints and omens.
The room in shadow, perhaps the wrong room?
The cockroach on the wall,
The naked lovers kissing
On the TV with the sound off.
I could hear the red faucet drip.

Or else restore to plain view
What is eternally invisible
And speaks by being silent.
Blue distances to the North,
The fires of the evening to the West,
Christ himself in pain, panhandling
On the altar of the storefront church
With a long bloody nail in each palm.

In this moment of amazement ...
Since I do ask for it humbly,
Without greed, out of true need.
My teeth chattered so loudly,
My old dog got up to see what's the matter.
Oh divine lassitude, long drawn-out sigh
As the vision came and went.

VIA DEL TRITONE

In Rome, on the street of that name,
I was walking alone in the sun
In the noonday heat, when I saw a house
With shutters closed, the sight of which
Pained me so much, I could have
Been born there and left inconsolably.

The ochre walls, the battered old door
I was tempted to push open and didn't,
Knowing already the coolness of the entrance,
The garden with a palm tree beyond,
And the dark stairs on the left.

Shutters closed to cool shadowy rooms
With impossibly high ceilings,
And here and there a watery mirror
And my pale and contorted face
To greet me and startle me again and again.

"You found what you were looking for,"
I expected someone to whisper.
But there was no one, neither there
Nor in the street, which was deserted
In that monstrous heat that gives birth
To false memories and tritons.

THE SECRET

I have my excuse, Mr. Death,
The old note my mother wrote
The day I missed school.
Snow fell. I told her my head hurt
And my chest. The clock struck
The hour. I lay in my father's bed
Pretending to be asleep.

Through the windows I could see
The snow-covered roofs. In my mind
I rode a horse; I was in a ship
On a stormy sea. Then I dozed off.
When I woke, the house was still.
Where was my mother?
Had she written the note and left?

I rose and went searching for her.
In the kitchen our white cat sat
Picking at the bloody head of a fish.
In the bathroom the tub was full,
The mirror and the window fogged over.

When I wiped them, I saw my mother
In her red bathrobe and slippers
Talking to a soldier on the street
While the snow went on falling,
And she put a finger
To her lips, and held it there.

From *Walking the Black Cat*, 1996

MIRRORS AT 4 A.M.

You must come to them sideways
In rooms webbed in shadow,
Sneak a view of their emptiness
Without them catching
A glimpse of you in return.

The secret is,
Even the empty bed is a burden to them,
A pretense.
They are more themselves keeping
The company of a blank wall,
The company of time and eternity

Which, begging your pardon,
Cast no image
As they admire themselves in the mirror,
While you stand to the side
Pulling a hanky out
To wipe your brow surreptitiously.

RELAXING IN A MADHOUSE

They had already attached the evening's tears to the windowpanes.

The general was busy with the ant farm in his head.

The holy saints in their tombs were burning, all except one who was a prisoner of a dark-haired movie star.

Moses wore a false beard and so did Lincoln.

X reproduced the Socratic method of interrogation by demonstrating the ceiling's ignorance.

"They stole the secret of the musical matchbook from me," confided Adam.

"The world's biggest rooster was going to make me famous," said Eve.

O to run naked over the darkening meadow after the cold shower!

In the white pavilion the nurse was turning water into wine.

Hurry home, dark cloud.

LATE CALL

A message for you,
Piece of shit:

You double-crossed us.
You were supposed to get yourself
Crucified
For the sake of Truth . . .

Who, me?

A mere crumb, thankfully,
Overlooked on a dinner table,
Lacking in enthusiasm . . .
An average nobody.

Oh, the worries . . .

In the dark windowpane
My mouth gutted open.
Aghast.
The panel of judges all black-hooded.

It must be a joke.
A misunderstanding, fellows.
A wrong number, surely?
A slipup?
An erratum?

EMILY'S THEME

My dear trees, I no longer recognize you
In this wintry light.
You brought me a reminder I can do without:
The world is old, it was always old,
There's nothing new in it this afternoon.
The garden could've been a padlocked window
Of a pawnshop I was studying
With every item in it dust-covered.

Each one of my thoughts was being ghostwritten
By anonymous authors. Each time they hit
A cobwebbed typewriter key, I shuddered.
Luckily, dark came quickly today.
Soon the neighbors were burning leaves,
And perhaps a few other things too.
Later, I saw the children run around the fire,
Their faces demonic in its flames.

CAMEO APPEARANCE

I had a small, nonspeaking part
In a bloody epic. I was one of the
Bombed and fleeing humanity.
In the distance our great leader
Crowed like a rooster from a balcony,
Or was it a great actor
Impersonating our great leader?

That's me there, I said to the kiddies.
I'm squeezed between the man
With two bandaged hands raised
And the old woman with her mouth open
As if she were showing us a tooth

That hurts badly. The hundred times
I rewound the tape, not once
Could they catch sight of me
In that huge gray crowd,
That was like any other gray crowd.

Trot off to bed, I said finally.
I know I was there. One take
Is all they had time for.
We ran, and the planes grazed our hair,
And then they were no more
As we stood dazed in the burning city,
But, of course, they didn't film that.

WHAT THE GYPSIES TOLD MY GRANDMOTHER
WHILE SHE WAS STILL A YOUNG GIRL

War, illness and famine will make you their favorite grandchild.
You'll be like a blind person watching a silent movie.
You'll chop onions and pieces of your heart
    into the same hot skillet.
Your children will sleep in a suitcase tied with a rope.
Your husband will kiss your breasts every night
    as if they were two gravestones.

Already the crows are grooming themselves
    for you and your people.
Your oldest son will lie with flies on his lips
    without smiling or lifting his hand.
You'll envy every ant you meet in your life
    and every roadside weed.
Your body and soul will sit on separate stoops
    chewing the same piece of gum.

Little cutie, are you for sale? the devil will say.
The undertaker will buy a toy for your grandson.
Your mind will be a hornet's nest even on your
    deathbed.
You will pray to God but God will hang a sign
    that He's not to be disturbed.
Question no further, that's all I know.

CHARM SCHOOL

Madame Gabrielle, were you really French?
And what were those heavy books
You made them balance on top of their heads,
Young women with secret aspirations
We saw strolling past the row of windows
In the large room above Guido's barbershop?

On the same floor was the office of an obscure
Weekly preaching bloody revolution.
Men with raised collars and roving eyes
Wandered in and out. When they conspired
They spat and pulled down the yellow shades,
Not to raise them or open the windows again

Until the summer heat came and your students
Wore dresses with their shoulders bared
As they promenaded with books on their heads,
And the bald customer in the barbershop
Sat sweating while overseeing in the mirror
His three remaining hairs being carefully combed.

OCTOBER LIGHT

That same light by which I saw her last
Made me close my eyes now in revery,
Remembering how she sat in the garden

With a red shawl over her shoulders
And a small book in her lap,
Once in a long while looking up

With the day's brightness on her face,
As if to appraise something of utmost seriousness
She has just read at least twice,

With the sky clear and open to view,
Because the leaves had already fallen
And lay still around her two feet.

GHOSTS

It's Mr. Brown looking much better
Than he did in the morgue.
He's brought me a huge carp
In a bloodstained newspaper.
What an odd visit.
I haven't thought of him in years.

Linda is with him and so is Sue.
Two pale and elegant fading memories
Holding each other by the hand.
Even their lipstick is fresh
Despite all the scientific proofs
To the contrary.

Is Linda going to cook the fish?
She turns and gazes in the direction
Of the kitchen while Sue
Continues to watch me mournfully.
I don't believe any of it,
And still I'm scared stiff.

I know of no way to respond,
So I do nothing.
The windows are open. The air's thick
With the scent of magnolias.
Drops of evening rain are dripping
From the dark and heavy leaves.
I take a deep breath; I close my eyes.

Dear specters, I don't even believe
You are here, so how is it
You're making me comprehend
Things I would rather not know just yet?

It's the way you stare past me
At what must already be my own ghost,
Before taking your leave,
As unexpectedly as you came in,
Without one of us breaking the silence.

AT THE COOKOUT

The wives of my friends
Have the air
Of having shared a secret.
Their eyes are lowered
But when we ask them
What for
They only glance at each other
And smile,
Which only increases our desire
To know ...

Something they did
Long ago,
Heedless of the consequences,
That left
Such a lingering sweetness?

Is that the explanation
For the way
They rest their chins
In the palms of their hands,
Their eyes closed
In the summer heat?

Come tell us,
Or give us a hint.
Trace a word or just a single letter
In the wine
Spilled on the table.

No reply. Both of them
Lovey-dovey
With the waning sunlight
And the evening breeze
On their faces.

The husbands drinking
And saying nothing,
Dazed and mystified as they are
By their wives' power
To give
And take away happiness,
As if their heads
Were crawling with snakes.

CLUB MIDNIGHT

Are you the sole owner of a seedy nightclub?

Are you its sole customer, sole bartender,
Sole waiter prowling around the empty tables?

Do you put on wee-hour girlie shows
With dead stars of black-and-white films?

Is your office upstairs over the neon lights,
Or down deep in the rat cellar?

Are bearded Russian thinkers your silent partners?
Do you have a doorman by the name of Dostoyevsky?

Is Fu Manchu coming tonight?
Is Miss Emily Dickinson?

Do you happen to have an immortal soul?
Do you have a sneaky suspicion that you have none?

Is that why you flip a white pair of dice,
In the dark, long after the joint closes?

BLOOD ORANGE

It looks so dark the end of the world may be near.
I believe it's going to rain.
The birds in the park are silent.
Nothing is what it seems to be,
Nor are we.

There's a tree on our street so big
We can all hide in its leaves.
We won't need any clothes either.
I feel as old as a cockroach, you said.
In my head, I'm a passenger on a ghost ship.

Not even a sigh outdoors now.
If a child was left on our doorstep,
It must be asleep.
Everything is teetering on the edge of everything
With a polite smile.

It's because there are things in this world
That just can't be helped, you said.
Right then, I heard the blood orange
Roll off the table and with a thud
Lie cracked open on the floor.

PASTORAL HARPSICHORD

A house with a screened-in porch
On the road to nowhere.
The missus topless because of the heat,
A bag of Frito Banditos in her lap.
President Bush on TV
Watching her every bite.

Poor reception, that's the one
Advantage we have here,
I said to the mutt lying at my feet
And sighing in sympathy.
On another channel the preacher
Came chaperoned by his ghost
When he shut his eyes full of tears
To pray for dollars.

"Bring me another beer," I said to her ladyship,
And when she wouldn't oblige,
I went out to make chamber music
Against the sunflowers in the yard.

THE FRIENDS OF HERACLITUS

Your friend has died, with whom
You roamed the streets,
At all hours, talking philosophy.
So, today you went alone,
Stopping often to change places
With your imaginary companion,
And argue back against yourself
On the subject of appearances:
The world we see in our heads
And the world we see daily,
So difficult to tell apart
When grief and sorrow bow us over.

You two often got so carried away
You found yourselves in strange neighborhoods
Lost among unfriendly folk,
Having to ask for directions
While on the verge of a supreme insight,
Repeating your question
To an old woman or a child
Both of whom may have been deaf and dumb.

What was that fragment of Heraclitus
You were trying to remember
As you stepped on the butcher's cat?
Meantime, you yourself were lost
Between someone's new black shoe
Left on the sidewalk

And the sudden terror and exhilaration
At the sight of a girl
Dressed up for a night of dancing
Speeding by on roller skates.

From *Jackstraws*, 1999

THE VOICE AT 3:00 A.M.

Who put canned laughter
Into my crucifixion scene?

SPECK-SIZED SCREAMING HEAD

Hoping to make yourself heard,
Mr. No-See?
Busting your balls
For one long, bloodcurdling scream,
Out of the dustheap
At my feet.

Fat chance. Someone's just putting
A quarter in the jukebox,
Someone else is starting the pink Cadillac convertible
On the street,
And I'm lifting and cocking the broom
In your direction.

THE SOUL HAS MANY BRIDES

In India I was greatly taken up
With a fly in a temple
Which gave me the distinct feeling
It was possible, just possible,
That we had met before.

Was it in Mexico City?
Climbing the blood-spotted, yellow legs
Of the crucified Christ
While his eyes grew larger and larger.
"May God seat you on the highest throne
Of his invisible Kingdom,"
A blind beggar said to me in English.
He knew what I saw.

At the saloon where Pancho Villa
Fired his revolvers at the ceiling,
On the bare ass of a naked nymph
Stepping out of a lake in a painting,
And now shamelessly crawling up
One of Buddha's nostrils,
Whose smile got even more secretive,
Even more squint-eyed.

EL LIBRO DE LA SEXUALIDAD

The pages of all the books are blank.
The late-night readers at the town library
Make no complaints about that.
They lift their heads solely
To consult the sign commanding silence,
Before they lick their fingers,
Look sly, appear to be dozing off,
As they pinch the corner of the paper
Ever-so-carefully,
While turning the heavy page.

In the yellow puddle of light,
Under the lamp with green shade,
The star charts are all white
In the big astronomy atlas
Lying open between my bare arms.
At the checkout desk, the young Betelgeuse
Is painting her lips red
Using my sweating forehead as a mirror.
Her roving tongue
Is a long-tailed comet in the night sky.

MUMMY'S CURSE

Befriending an eccentric young woman,
The sole resident of a secluded Victorian mansion.
She takes long walks in the evening rain,
And so do I, with my hair full of dead leaves.

In her former life, she was an opera singer.
She remembers the rich Neapolitan pastries,
Points to a bit of fresh whipped cream
Still left in the corner of her lower lip,
Tells me she dragged a wooden cross once
Through a leper town somewhere in India.

I was born in Copenhagen, I confide in turn.
My father was a successful mortician.
My mother never lifted her nose out of a book.
Arthur Schopenhauer ruined our happy home.
Since then, a day doesn't go by without me
Sticking a loaded revolver inside my mouth.

She had walked ahead of me and had turned
Like a lion tamer, towering with a whip in hand.
Luckily, in that moment, the mummy sped by
On a bicycle carrying someone's pizza order
And cursing the mist and the potholes.

PRISON GUARDS SILHOUETTED
AGAINST THE SKY

I never gave them a thought. Years had gone by.
Many years. I had plenty of other things
To worry about. Today I was in the dentist's chair
When his new assistant walked in
Pretending not to recognize me in the slightest
As I opened my mouth most obediently.

We were necking in some bushes by the riverbank,
And I wanted her to slip off her bra.
The sky was darkening, there was thunder
When she finally did, so that the first large
Raindrop wet one of her brown nipples.

That was nicer than what she did to my mouth now,
While I winced, while I waited for a wink,
A burst of laughter at the memory of the two of us
Buttoning ourselves, running drenched
Past the state prison with its armed guards
Silhouetted in their towers against the sky.

SCHOOL FOR VISIONARIES

The teacher sits with eyes closed.
When you play chess alone it's always your move.
I'm in the last row with a firefly in the palm of my hand.
The girl with red braids, who saw the girl with red braids?

*

Do you believe in something truer than truth?
Do you prick your ears even when you know damn well
    no one is coming?
Does that explain the lines on your forehead?
Your invisible friend, what happened to her?

*

The rushing wind slides to a stop to listen.
The prisoner opens the thick dictionary lying on his knees.
The floor is cold and his feet are bare.
A chew-toy of the gods, is that him?

*

Do you stare and stare at every black windowpane
As if it were a photo of your unsmiling parents?
Are you homesick for the house of cards?
The sad late-night cough, is it yours?

MIDSUMMER FEAST

for Michael Ferber

Here I am then, nearly blind in both eyes,
Half-deaf, half-lame,
Touched in the head, frothing at the mouth,
A fearful, shrinking worm
Crawling in your carcass, oh mystery,
Raising hell, chewing you out.

My hunch is, you prefer to remain forever
Unthinkable and unsayable,
Merely delectable, so that I may continue
To sate myself on your sweet appearances,
Your luscious, flower-strewn meadows,
Your vast banquets of evening stars.

OBSCURELY OCCUPIED

You are the Lord of the maimed,
The one bled and crucified
In a cellar of some prison
Over which the day is breaking.

You inspect the latest refinements
Of cruelty. You may even kneel
Down in wonder. They know
Their business, these grim fellows

Whose wives and mothers rise
For the early Mass. You, yourself,
Must hurry back through the snow
Before they find your rightful

Place on the cross vacated,
The few candles burning higher
In your terrifying absence
Under the darkly magnified dome.

ON THE MEADOW

With the wind gusting so wildly,
So unpredictably,
I'm willing to bet one or two ants
May have tumbled on their backs
As we sit here on the porch.

Their feet are pedaling
Imaginary bicycles.
It's a battle of wits against
Various physical laws,
Plus Fate, plus—
So-what-else-is-new?

Wondering if anyone's coming to their aid
Bringing cake crumbs,
Miniature editions of the Bible,
A lost thread or two
Cleverly tied end to end.

TALKING TO THE CEILING

The moths rustle the pages of the evening papers.

A beautiful sleepwalker terrorizes Kansas.

Cannibal waiter ate two of his diners.

I was snooping on myself, pointing the long finger.

Whose orange hairpiece is that? the cop said.

All of creation, you are in my bad books.

I'm always thinking of you, Margie.

If only I had a paper crown on my head.

I'd play tapes of your inspired snoring.

The big question, can we continue

To keep the grim reaper laughing?

The long menu of mouthwatering misfortunes

Lies scrawled in the palms of our hands.

Unknown namesake in a roach motel, go to sleep.

Please cut the cards with eyes closed.

A hundred horror films in my head.

A baby smuggled inside a watermelon.

Madame Zaza stays open late.

Hangman's convention: ropemaker's workshop.

Do you have fears you'll be crushed by an ant?

In Charon's ferryboat, I aim to give ladies my seat.

It's just the way I've been brought up.

Mr. Salesman, would these shoes look good in my coffin?

The masked intruder with a dollhouse knife was her!

I'll try going beddie-bye in a saddle.

Naked truth, you've got to see the boobs on her!

In my youth boys used to light farts in the dark.

The insomniac's brain is a choo-choo train.

Cassandra with a plastic rose between her teeth.

Is this the cabinet of Dr. Caligari?

Who is that milking a black goat under the blanket?

Like a master criminal dodging his sleeplessness

I sleep in a different bed every night.

John Calvin, stick to your knitting!

The general never came out of the closet

Because he could not find the beach ball.

My love's ill luck was in love with my ill luck.

The goldfish helped me through many a bad night.

Hair by hair we were circumnavigating my head.

Have I been made the official match vendor

Of the great dark night of the soul?

Waiting for the sunrise, the pink birthday cake!

*

The hurricane century tossed my bed around.

Two tumbleweeds on a pillow, we raced for cover.

A candlelight dinner in the Nevada desert.

Here, throw my red hat into the lion cage,

The lady in the zoo said to her crying son.

Oh, to press the chimney to my heart on a windy day!

The air sultry, the ice melting in the glasses.

My clock belonged to Queen Persephone herself.

She spent her nights stuffing anchovies into olives.

Coming down from the trees was a big mistake.

The colonel praised the moderate use of electric shocks.

Selling sticks of gum door-to-door in my old age.

Small-beer metaphysician, King of birdshit!

I growled at the mirror till it turned its back on me.

The pitcher on TV stopped in the middle of his windup.

When I bump my head against the wall,

I am the first to offer sincere apologies.

The undercover agent under my covers stayed hidden.

To pass the time, I played a teensy fiddle

Using one of my love's long black eyelashes as a bow.

Remember me, folks.

Girls were already thumbing their noses at me in 1944.

Oh memory, making us all get out and push your hearse!

In calmest tones, I inquired about hell's cuisine

From the worm endeavoring to crawl inside my ear.

A dive with dim lights and middle-aged waitress.

She kept writing my order in elaborate scrawl

Till the clock coughed up its first drop of blood.

Memory, all-night's bedside tattoo artist.

Tell them Death, tell them that yourself.

On the gallows I'll be offering to pick up the check.

Quick, a telescope for a peek inside my head!

Murk extraordinaire, flying rat heaven.

Pray to chance Simic, the jokester in the deck!

And what exactly are these noises in my ear?

Her last lover hid under the bed for years

While she kept a quiet, shady armpit and crotch

For me to snuggle in after lunch in the garden.

And to think, I once rode the dragon-headed ship

On the merry-go-round in the heart of Texas!

Eternity, dim-lit hallway in a skid-row hotel,

My future is my past, the scratchy record sang.

Father of the universe, what wine do you sip?

With tiny love bites she ate my heart.

Didn't want the salt and pepper I offered.

Long hours of the night; St. John of the Cross

And Blaise Pascal the cops in a patrol car.

Do you have a favorite black hole in heaven?

The fleeting moments know no care.

Every day I discover serious new obstacles

To my guaranteed pursuit of happiness.

There was a funeral in my coffee cup tonight.

I'm not just *any* black flea on your ass!

I shouted to every god I could think of.

Infinity's ink has spilled over me

And left me badly smudged.

What could be causing all this, Madam and sir?

The old blues, the kind you never lose.

I'm just a poor boy a long way from home.

Prison and orphanage taught me how to play.

My love, feeling around for a lost hairpin,

I can imagine you smiling at my nonsense.

There are flyers on the floor

Addressed to the Occupant.

There are a million zeros crowding for warmth

Inside my head and making it so heavy.

Do you hear them multiplying in the dark?

The one called Jesus turning up scared

To ask to sleep in a murderer's bed.

Little rain, keep on falling softly.

DE OCCULTA PHILOSOPHIA

Evening sunlight,
Your humble servant
Seeks initiation
Into your occult ways.

Out of the late-summer sky,
Its deepening quiet,
You brought me a summons,
A small share in some large
And obscure knowledge.

Tell me something of your study
Of lengthening shadows,
The blazing windowpanes
Where the soul is turned into light—
Or don't just now.

You have the air of someone
Who prefers to dwell in solitude,
The one who enters, with gravity
Of mien and imposing severity,
A room suddenly rich in enigmas.

Oh supreme unknowable,
The seemingly inviolable reserve
Of your stratagems
Makes me quake at the thought
Of you finding me thus

Seated in a shadowy back room
At the edge of a village
Bloodied by the setting sun,
To tell me so much,
To tell me absolutely nothing.

MYSTIC LIFE

lifetime's solitary thread

  for Charles Wright

It's like fishing in the dark,
If you ask me:
Our thoughts are the hooks,
Our hearts the raw bait.

We cast the line over our heads,
Past all believing,
Into the starless midnight sky,
Until it's lost to sight.

The line's long unraveling
Rising in our throats like a sigh
Of a long day's weariness,
Soul-searching and revery.

     *

One little thought against
The supreme unthinkable.

How about that?

Mr. Looney Tunes fishing in the dark
Out of an empty sleeve
With a mourning band on it.

The fly and the spider on the ceiling
Looking on, brother.

*

In the high school of hide-and-seek,

In its vast classroom
Of smoke and mirrors,
Where we are the twin dunces
Left standing in
The darkest corner.

Our fates in the mouth
Of the one
Who hath no image,
Glistening there
As if moistened by his tongue.

*

It takes a tiny nibble
From time to time.

Don't you believe it.

It sends a shiver down our spines
In response.

Like hell it does.

There's a door you've never noticed before
Left ajar in your room.

Don't kid yourself.

The song said: *Do nothing*
Till you hear from me.

Yes, of course.

In the meantime,

Wear mirror-tinted
Glasses to bed.
Say in your prayers:
In that thou hast sought me,
Thou hast already found me.

That's what the leaves
Are all upset about tonight.

*

Solitary fishermen
Lining up like zeros—

To infinity.

Lying in the shade
Chewing on the bitter verb
"To be."
The ripple of the abyss
Closing in on them.

Therein the mystery
And the pity.

The hook left dangling
In the Great "Nothing,"

Surely snipped off
By XXXXXX's own
Moustache-trimming scissors . . .

Nevertheless, aloft,

White shirttails and all—

I'll be damned!

AMBIGUITY'S WEDDING

for E.D.

Bride of Awe, all that's left for us
Are vestiges of a feast table,
Levitating champagne glasses
In the hands of the erased millions.

Mr. So-and-So, the bridegroom
Of absent looks, lost looks,
The pale reporter from the awful doors
Before our identity was leased.

At night's delicious close,
A few avatars of mystery still about,
The spider at his trade,
The print of his vermillion foot on my hand.

A faded woman in sallow dress
Gravely smudged, her shadow on the wall
Becoming visible, a wintry shadow
Quieter than sleep.

Soul, take thy risk.
There where your words and thoughts
Come to a stop,
Encipher me thus, in marriage.

HEAD OF A DOLL

Whose demon are you,
Whose god? I asked
Of the painted mouth
Half buried in the sand.

A brooding gull
Made a brief assessment,
And tiptoed away
Nodding to himself.

At dusk a firefly or two
Dowsed its eye pits.
And later, toward midnight,
I even heard mice.

From *Night Picnic*, 2001

PAST-LIVES THERAPY

They explained to me the bloody bandages
On the floor in the maternity ward in Rochester, N.Y.,
Cured the backache I acquired bowing to my old master,
Made me stop putting thumbtacks round my bed.

They showed me an officer on horseback,
Waving a saber next to a burning farmhouse
And a barefoot woman in a nightgown,
Throwing stones after him and calling him Lucifer.

I was a straw-headed boy in patched overalls.
Come dark a chicken would roost in my hair.
Some even laid eggs as I played my ukulele
And my mother and father crossed themselves.

Next, I saw myself inside an abandoned gas station
Constructing a spaceship out of a coffin,
Red traffic cone, cement mixer and ear warmers,
When a church lady fainted seeing me in my underwear.

Some days, however, they opened door after door,
Always to a different room, and could not find me.
There'd be only a small squeak now and then,
As if a miner's canary got caught in a mousetrap.

UNMADE BEDS

They like shady rooms,
Peeling wallpaper,
Cracks on the ceiling,
Flies on the pillow.

If you are tempted to lie down,
Don't be surprised,
You won't mind the dirty sheets,
The rasp of rusty springs
As you make yourself comfy.
The room is a darkened movie theater
Where a grainy,
Black-and-white film is being shown.

A blur of disrobed bodies
In the moment of sweet indolence
That follows lovemaking,
When the meanest of hearts
Comes to believe
Happiness can last forever.

STREET OF JEWELERS

What each one of these hundreds
Of windows did with the gold
That was melting in them this morning,
I cannot begin to imagine.

I act like a prospective burglar,
Noting the ones that are open,
Their curtains drawn to the side
By someone stark naked
I may have just missed.

Here, where no one walks now,
And when he does, he goes softly,
So as not to tip the scales
In the act of weighing
Specks of dust in the dying sunlight.

THE ONE TO WORRY ABOUT

I failed miserably at imagining nothing.
Something always came to keep me company:
A small nameless bug crossing the table,
The memory of my mother, the ringing in my ear.
I was distracted and perplexed.
A hole is invariably a hole in something.

About seven this morning, a lone beggar
Waited for me with his small, sickly dog,
Whose eyes grew bigger on seeing me.
There goes, the eyes said, that nice man
To whom (appearances to the contrary)
Nothing in this whole wide world is sacred.

I was still a trifle upset entering the bakery
When an unknown woman stepped out
Of the back to wait on me dressed for a night
On the town in a low-cut, tight-fitting black dress.
Her face was solemn, her eyes averted,
While she placed a muffin in my hand,
As if all along she knew what I was thinking.

CHERRY BLOSSOM TIME

Gray sewage bubbling up out of street sewers
After the spring rain with the clear view
Of hawkers of quack remedies and their customers
Swarming on the Capitol steps.

At the National Gallery the saints' tormented faces
Suddenly made sense.
Several turned their eyes on me
As I stepped over the shiny parquetry.

And who and what was I, if you please?
A minor provincial grumbler on a holiday,
With hands clasped behind his back
Nodding to everyone he meets

As if this were a 1950s Fall of the Roman Empire movie set,
And we the bewildered,
Absurdly costumed, milling extras
Among the pink cherry blossoms.

SUNDAY PAPERS

The butchery of the innocent
Never stops. That's about all
We can ever be sure of, love,
Even than the roast
You are bringing out of the oven.

It's Sunday. The congregation
Files slowly out of the church
Across the street. A good many
Carry Bibles in their hands.
It's the vague desire for truth
And the mighty fear of it
That makes them turn up
Despite the glorious spring weather.

In the hallway, the old mutt
Just now had the honesty
To growl at his own image in the mirror,
Before lumbering off to the kitchen
Where the lamb roast sat
In your outstretched hands
Smelling of garlic and rosemary.

AND THEN I THINK

I'm just a storefront dentist
Extracting a blackened tooth at midnight.

I chewed on many bitter truths, Doc,
My patient says after he spits the blood out,

Still slumped over, gray-haired
And smelling of carrion just like me.

Of course, I may be the only one here,
And this is a mirror trick I'm performing.

Even the few small crumpled bills
He leaves on the way out, I don't believe in.

I may pluck them with a pair of wet pincers
And count them, and then I may not.

THE ALTAR

The plastic statue of the Virgin
On top of a bedroom dresser
With a blackened mirror
From a bad-dream grooming salon.

Two pebbles from the grave of a rock star,
A small, grinning wind-up monkey,
A bronze Egyptian coin
And a red movie-ticket stub.

A splotch of sunlight on the framed
Communion photograph of a boy
With the eyes of someone
Who will drown in a lake real soon.

An altar dignifying the god of chance.
What is beautiful, it cautions,
Is found accidentally and not sought after.
What is beautiful is easily lost.

MY FATHER ATTRIBUTED IMMORTALITY TO WAITERS

for Derek Walcott

For surely, there's no difficulty in understanding
The unreality of an occasional customer
Such as ourselves seated at one of the many tables
As pale as the cloth that covers them.

Time in its augmentations and diminutions
Does not concern these two in the least.
They stand side by side facing the street,
Wearing identical white jackets and fixed smiles,

Ready to incline their heads in welcome
Should one of us come through the door
After reading the high-priced menu on this street
Of many hunched figures and raised collars.

VIEWS FROM A TRAIN

Then there's aesthetic paradox
Which notes that someone else's tragedy
Often strikes the casual viewer
With the feeling of happiness.

There was the sight of squatters' shacks,
Naked children and lean dogs running
On what looked like a town dump,
The smallest one hopping after them on crutches.

All of a sudden we were in a tunnel.
The wheels ground our thoughts
Back and forth as if they were gravel.
Before long we found ourselves on a beach,
The water blue, the sky cloudless.

Seaside villas, palm trees, white sand;
A woman in a red bikini waved to us
As if she knew each one of us
Individually and was sorry to see us
Heading so quickly into another tunnel.

NIGHT PICNIC

There was the sky, starless and vast—
Home of every one of our dark thoughts—
Its door open to more darkness.
And you, like a late door-to-door salesman,
With only your own beating heart
In the palm of your outstretched hand.

All things are imbued with God's being—
(She said in hushed tones
As if his ghost might overhear us)
The dark woods around us,
Our faces, which we cannot see,
Even this bread we are eating.

You were mulling over the particulars
Of your cosmic insignificance
Between slow sips of red wine.
In the ensuing quiet, you could hear
Her small, sharp teeth chewing the crust—
And then, finally, she moistened her lips.

CAR GRAVEYARD

This is where all our joyrides ended:
Our fathers at the wheel, our mothers
With picnic baskets on their knees
As we sat in the back with our mouths open.

We were driving straight into the sunrise.
The country was flat. A city rose before us,
Its windows burning with the setting sun.
All that vanished as we quit the highway
And rolled down a dusky meadow
Strewn with beer cans and candy wrappers,
Till we came to a stop beside an old Ford.

First the radio preacher lost his voice,
Then our four tires went flat.
The springs popped out of the upholstery
Like alarmed rattlesnakes,
As we tried to remain calm.
Later that night we heard giggles
Out of a junked hearse—then, not a peep
Till the day of the Resurrection.

WOODEN CHURCH

It's just a boarded-up shack with a steeple
Under the blazing summer sky
On a back road seldom traveled
Where the shadows of tall trees
Graze peacefully like a row of gallows,
And crows with no carrion in sight
Caw to each other of better days.

The congregation may still be at prayer.
Farm folk from flyspecked photos
Standing in rows with their heads bowed
As if listening to your approaching steps.
So slow they are, you must be asking yourself
How come we are here one minute
And in the very next gone forever?

Try the locked door, then knock once.
The crows will stay out of sight.
High above you, there is the leaning spire
Still feeling the blow of the last storm.
And then the silence of the afternoon ...
Even the unbeliever must feel its force.

THE LIVES OF THE ALCHEMISTS

The great labor was always to efface oneself,
Reappear as something entirely different:
The pillow of a young woman in love,
A ball of lint pretending to be a spider.

Black boredoms of rainy country nights
Thumbing the writings of illustrious adepts
Offering advice on how to proceed with the transmutation
Of a figment of time into eternity.
The true master, one of them counseled,
Needs a hundred years to perfect his art.

In the meantime, the small arcana of the frying pan,
The smell of olive oil and garlic wafting
From room to empty room, the black cat
Rubbing herself against your bare leg
While you shuffle toward the distant light
And the tinkle of glasses in the kitchen.

New Poems

NEAREST NAMELESS

So damn familiar
Most of the time,
I don't even know you are here.
My life,
My portion of eternity,

A little shiver,
As if the chill of the grave
Is already
Catching up with me—
No matter.

Descartes smelled
Witches burning
While he sat thinking
Of a truth so obvious
We keep failing to see it.

I never knew it either
Till today.
When I heard a bird shriek:
The cat is coming,
And I felt myself tremble.

EMPTY BARBERSHOP

In pursuit of happiness, you may yet
Draw close to it momentarily
In one of these two leather-bound chairs
With the help of scissors and a comb,

Draped to the chin with a long white sheet,
While your head slips through
The invisible barber's greasy fingers
Making your hair stand up straight,

While he presses the razor to your throat,
Causing your eyes to spring open
As you discern in the mirror before you
The full length of the empty barbershop

With two vacant chairs and past them
The street, commensurately empty,
Except for the pressed and blurred face
Of someone straining to look inside.

IN THE STREET

Beauty, dark goddess,

We met and parted
As though we parted not.

Like two stopped watches
In a dusty store window,

One golden morning of time.

GRAYHEADED SCHOOLCHILDREN

Old men have bad dreams,
So they sleep little.
They walk on bare feet
Without turning on the lights,
Or they stand leaning
On gloomy furniture
Listening to their hearts beat.

The one window across the room
Is black like a blackboard.
Every old man is alone
In this classroom, squinting
At that fine chalk line
That divides being-here
From being-here-no-more.

No matter. It was a glass of water
They were going to get,
But not just yet.
They listen for mice in the walls,
A car passing on the street,
Their dead fathers shuffling past them
On their way to the kitchen.

SERVING TIME

Another dreary day in time's invisible
Penitentiary, making license plates
With lots of zeros, walking lockstep counter-
Clockwise in the exercise yard or watching
The lights dim when some poor fellow,
Who could as well be me, gets fried.

Here on death row, I read a lot of books.
First it was law, as you'd expect.
Then came history, ancient and modern.
Finally philosophy—all that being and nothingness stuff.
The more I read, the less I understand.
Still, other inmates call me professor.

Did I mention that we had no guards?
It's a closed book who locks
And unlocks the cell doors for us.
Even the executions we carry out
By ourselves, attaching the wires,
Playing warden, playing chaplain

All because a little voice in our head
Whispers something about our last appeal
Being denied by God himself.
The others hear nothing, of course,
But that, typically, you may as well face it,
Is how time runs things around here.

POSTCARD FROM S.

So far I've met here two Homers and one Virgil.
The town is like a living anthology of classic literature.
Thunder and lightning almost every afternoon.
When neighbors meet, they slap mosquitoes
On each other's foreheads and go off red in the face.

I'm lying in a hammock next to a burning barn
Watching a birch tree in the yard.
One minute it wrestles with the wind and smoke,
The next it raises its fists to curse the gods.
That, of course, makes it a Trojan
To the Greeks just arriving on a fire engine.

LITTLE NIGHT MUSIC

Of neighbors' voices and dishes
Being cleared away
On long summer evenings
With the windows open
As we sat on the back stairs,
Smoking and sipping beer.

The memory of that moment,
So sweet at first,
The two of us chatting away,
Till the stars made us quiet.
We drew close
And held fast to each other
As if in sudden danger.

That one time, I didn't recognize
Your voice, or dare turn
To look at your face
As you spoke of us being born
With so little apparent cause.
I could think of nothing to say.
The music over, the night cold.

DRIVING THESE ROADS

What good does it do you
To complain, Charles.
The fates shuffling the cards
Are old and blind.
You may as well look for them
In every nursing home in Tennessee.

One day your car breaks down
Outside some dead mill town
With a couple smokestacks in the rain,
And you trudge past the home
With your gasoline can in hand,
Almost brushing against the gray bricks

Just as the oldest one of them
Puts on her rhinestone glasses
To read what the cards have to say
Now that you are soaked wet
And are about to shiver to death,
Except it isn't your time yet.

THE MUSEUM OPENS AT MIDNIGHT

That's why only a couple of people wait outside.
They are strangers and the shadows of columns obscure them
    even further.
The windows across the avenue are no longer lit.
Everyone else must be asleep or nearly so.
The guard will be along any moment with the keys,
Or he may have come already and unlocked the doors.

At this late hour, they keep the museum dark,
Relying on lit candles in paintings to provide the light.
The Egyptian death masks are waiting.
The statues of naked Greek goddesses
And the Dutch interiors with canopied marriage beds.
You expect the couple to keep close together, but no.
She's off to another wing where there is a show
Of black-and-white photographs of small children
And he wants to see the martyrs in their torments.

It's up to us to divine what happens next.
The woman has found a bench to sit on.
She can't see the photos, but she believes she hears
The rustle of the girls' stiff dresses
As they stir slightly before the hooded camera.

Miraculously, the man has been able to discern
The pale sky above some saint's head.
Dawn is breaking, clouds are racing in the sky
While they get ready to torment him.
His eyes, turned heavenward, remain invisible,
And so do his bleeding wounds
Despite all the red paint the painter had used.

In truth, I've no idea what became of the couple.
The museum has a number of paintings
With distant hillside towns no one ever notices.
They may be in one them, alone or together,
Hugging the walls of narrow, winding streets,
And then, they may not be there at all
Or for that matter anywhere else I can think of.

PARTY FIEND

Pitch dark, as I poke around at an address
I had scribbled earlier at a party
Using a girl's bare back
To write the street and the number
While she kept tittering to herself.

In any case, here I am worrying about
How many matches I dare waste
Reading the names over the mailboxes.
I thought of ringing a random bell,
Saw them all already gathered upstairs,
Standing close and listening.

The bells made no sound. No door opened.
No hostess came down in a party dress
Carrying a glass of wine for me.
I had let the taxi go and had no idea where I was.
I had a choice of hurrying off
Or staying where I was a little longer

In the quiet moments before dawn,
With not a single lit window anywhere.
The graying sky barely visible.
One solitary birdcall, and then another,
Softer one, in response, here where
There were no trees or bushes in sight.

THE PROMPTER

The one who had been whispering
All along in this empty theater
And whose voice I just heard—
Or imagined I did
Distracted as I was by my own thoughts.

God have mercy on my poor soul
Was to be my line,
Which I couldn't bring myself to say
With shivers going up my spine
Like white mice.

And when I finally did get around to it,
There was no response.
A clap, someone chuckling briefly
Is all I had hoped for
And not this great sweep of nothing.

AUTUMN SKY

In my great-grandmother's time,
All one needed was a broom
To get to see places
And give the geese a chase in the sky.

*

The stars know everything,
So we try to read their minds.
As distant as they are,
We choose to whisper in their presence.

*

Oh, Cynthia,
Take a clock that has lost its hands
For a ride.
Get me a room at Hotel Eternity
Where Time likes to stop now and then.

*

Come, lovers of dark corners,
The sky says,
And sit in one of my dark corners.
There are tasty little zeros
In the peanut dish tonight.

SOMETHING LARGE IS IN THE WOODS

That's what the leaves are telling us tonight.
Hear them frighten and be struck dumb
So that we sit up listening to nothing,
Which is always more worrisome than something.

The minutes crawl like dog fleas up our legs.
We must wait for whatever it is to identify itself
In some as-yet-unspecified way
As the trees are rushing to warn us again,

The branches beat against the house to be let in,
And then change their minds abruptly.
Think how many leaves are holding still in the woods
With no wish to add to their troubles

With something so large closing upon us?
It makes one feel vaguely heroic
Sitting so late with no light in the house
And the night dark and starless out there.

TO THE ONE TUNNELING

Penitentiaries secured for the night,
Thousands lying awake in them,
As we too lie awake, love,
Straining to hear beyond the quiet.
The blurry whiteness at the ceiling
Of our darkened room like a sheet
Thrown over a body in the ice-cold morgue.

Do you hear the one tunneling?
So faint a sound he makes
It could be your heartbeat or mine
In this wall we lean our heads against.
With our eyes now tightly shut
As if a jailer has stopped to peek
Through the small crack in our door.

SEPARATE TRUTHS

Night fell without asking
For our permission.
Mary had a headache,
And my eyes hurt
From squinting at the newspapers.

We could still make out
A few old trees in the yard.
They take it as it comes.
Separate truths
Do not interest them.

We'll have to run for it, I said,
And had no idea what I meant.
The coming of the inevitable,
What a strange bliss that is,
And I had no idea what she meant.

THE SECRET DOCTRINE

Psst, psst, psst,
Is what the snow is saying
To the quiet woods,
With the night falling.

Something pressing,
That can't wait,
On a path that went nowhere,
Where I found myself

Overtaken by snow flakes
With so much to confide.
The bare twigs pricked their ears—
Great God!

What did they say?
What did they say?
I went badgering
Every tree and bush.

THE HEARSE

for G.

Your hearse pulled by fortune-teller's white mice
Pulled by your mother and father
Pulled by the wind and rain
Pulled by teenage Jesus already carrying his cross
Pulled by your first love
Pulled by every dog you ever owned
Pulled by the fly whose legs you plucked

*

A hearse like a rain-streaked telephone booth
Full of fire-sale leaflets
The receiver off the hook
A hiss as if a record had just ended
Some happy song played sadly
Your shirttails sticking out of a rear gate
Trying to make their getaway

You crawled out of your hearse
To help a fallen horse to his feet
Rows of sugar maples lined the road
Necessity the old coachman held the reins
A crow like a defrocked priest sat by his side
The hearse with whorehouse curtains

★

It's a ghost ship and on that ship
A pool table where you'll play snooker
With three veiled women
Everything is made of light even the dark night
The candles whisper
As they draw close to watch
The great nothing hoard its winnings

CAFÉ DON QUIXOTE

Trees like country preachers
On their rostrums,
Their arms raised in blessing
Over the evening fields.
Every leaf now, every weed
Helping the night
Darken and quiet the world
For what's to come.

Birds of a feather, listen,
Pay attention to me.
I'm setting out astride my phantom Rozinante.
Down a winding road where crows vanish.
Imponderabilia, wherever you're hiding,
Hop in the saddle with me.

No two blades of grass, no two shadows
Whisper our names alike.
CAFÉ DON QUIXOTE in blood-red neon
Just now coming into view
In the vast, dark-clouded,
Storm-threatening West.

Some of the new poems have been published in the following magazines, to whose editors grateful acknowledgment is given: *London Review of Books, The Iowa Review, Poetry Ireland, Raritan, The Yale Review, The New Yorker.*

LATE SEPTEMBER

The mail truck goes down the coast
Carrying a single letter.
At the end of a long pier
The bored seagull lifts a leg now and then
And forgets to put it down.
There is a menace in the air
Of tragedies in the making.

Last night you thought you heard television
In the house next door.
You were sure it was some new
Horror they were reporting,
So you went out to find out.
Barefoot, wearing just shorts.
It was only the sea sounding weary
After so many lifetimes
Of pretending to be rushing off somewhere
And never getting anywhere.

This morning, it felt like Sunday.
The heavens did their part
By casting no shadow along the boardwalk
Or the row of vacant cottages,
Among them a small church
With a dozen gray tombstones huddled close
As if they, too, had the shivers.